DANCE IDEAS

DANCE IDEAS

for Teachers, Students and Children

Kate Harrison·John Auty

Hodder & Stoughton

LONDON SYDNEY AUCKLAND

British Library Cataloguing in Publication Data
Harrison, Kate
 Dance ideas for teachers, students and children.
 1. Dancing
 I. Title II. Auty, John
 792.8

 ISBN 0 340 42770 1

First published 1991
Impression number   10 9 8 7 6 5 4 3
Year   1998 1997 1996 1995 1994 1993

Typeset by Litho Link Ltd, Welshpool, Wales.
Printed in Great Britain for the educational publishing division
of Hodder & Stoughton Ltd, Mill Road, Dunton Green, Sevenoaks,
Kent TN13 2YA by Thomson Litho Ltd, East Kilbride.

Contents

Introduction   7

Section 1   21
   Into action – the body

Section 2   43
   Shaping the action – space

Section 3   57
   Colouring the action – dynamics

Section 4   73
   Making the action – choreography

Conclusion   107

Useful books   109

Acknowledgments   111

Introduction

The reasons for writing this book are very simple. Firstly, a need to give expression to a set of basic beliefs developed through time and circumstance which are fundamental to a good dance education. Secondly, a desire to share with others a number of dance ideas, unrelated to age or stage of development, that have inherent simplicity and quality.

Let us start with quality first. Quality by definition means distinctive, equating to a high degree of excellence. Whatever the end result of any dance work, the outcome at every stage should be quality. If this is the objective, then an end product recognised as having quality can only be achieved if the initial idea is one of quality also. Logically this must be supported right the way through every stage of development, from beginning to conclusion, by exercising basic elements, processes, procedures and practices of equal quality as far as is humanly possible. This means good organisation and planning, thorough research, attention to detail, a sound work ethic, and an uncompromising high expectation level. Bound tightly to this structure should be a continuum running from caring and careful at one end, to demanding and ruthless at the other.

The quest for quality in dance is an ongoing process which is constantly changing according to the age, experience and aptitudes of both teacher and dancer. So, what is quality and how can it be nurtured, trained and developed?

Quality in dance is easily observed. You do not need a dance background to know when a dancer produces quality in both the technical and expressive aspects of the act. So, what makes up qualitative action and how can you strive to improve the quality of the dancers, and the quality of your or their dance compositions?

Dancers constantly strive to perfect their bodies in order to gain extra strength and a greater degree of control. In this way their bodies become trained to be instruments of quality. However, quality in dance terms is more than training. It can be observed in the stretch of the foot . . . the bend of the body . . the focus beyond the gesture . . . the astonishing balance . . . the leap which soars . . . and through numerous other incredible body activities.

The quality of the dance is very important to the maker of dances. It can be achieved only by demanding more, and expecting an improved performance level at every dance session. The quest for quality is therefore the ultimate responsibility of the dance makers. Always aim for more, even more than you ever envisaged possible when your dance idea was first conceived. The dance requires more, to gain complete quality.

It requires underpinning by a technique whether formal or informal. A language by which to communicate has to be achieved, and this means developing a vocabulary of movement good enough to articulate the expression. This can only be brought about by experimentation and exploration – improvisation in other words. Emotion, intellect and body language are required to fuse so that the most extraordinary athletic and aesthetic feats are possible because they are performed as part of the overall expression of the dance. This is good news for the novice with no previous dance training or knowledge. Some of the best examples of quality are to be found in innocent, uninhibited actions and phrases. Once all the parts are ordered, by juxtaposing if necessary until a statement is composed, the choreography becomes manifest.

> *Technique is the routine . . .*
> *Movement is the language . . .*
> *Improvisation is the method . . .*
> *Choreography should be the result . . .*
> *Quality is the goal.*

The routine

Good dance practice requires a number of basic routines which occur as a matter of course, in a matter–of–fact way. They are as regular as clockwork and become so internalised that they are second nature – yet another of a dancer's umpteenth senses beyond the traditional five! What are they you ask? Technique in its widest interpretation; the ability to find and use space; being able to trust and to be trusted; coming to terms with fear and the structure, or shape, of the dance session. Let us take them one at a time, for they represent very basic elements of good dance teaching and learning.

Technique

Dance technique prepares the body for dancing. This simple tenet cannot be ignored and should not be avoided. It is the right of anyone who wishes to explore their movement potential to gain strength, flexibility and coordination and thus become more responsive, articulate and sensitised as the range of their body's capabilities is extended. The need for regular warm-up gives the opportunity for enlarging the young dancer's vocabulary of movement, for disciplining the mind, and for learning the skills needed to gain control of the body as an instrument of movement creation. It should never be used as an end in itself.

But what do we mean by dance technique? Without wishing to dwell on the matter, or rehearse arguments that have raged over the years, it can range from a known and formally recognised technique to original exercises created with and according to the needs and abilities of the individual group being taught. What is important is not what, or whose, the dance technique is, but that it be introduced and be in use at the beginning of every session every time, so that systematically the skills it offers are available to be learned.

If only five minutes is available in any one session, it doesn't matter – the warm-up must happen. Not only that, it must be a balanced warm-up. The cycle of floor to standing to travel should be followed, again, regardless of the amount of time available. Without the routine of the cycle being completed, the exercising is incomplete and the technique session or warm-up cannot serve its function. Incidentally, the cycle symbolically reinforces the important concepts of beginning, middle, and end, and of making progression. To maintain what the body can already do is not enough. It has to be able to do more.

All truly creative work, whether it be in words, pictures, sculpture, music, drama, or dance has technique behind it. We can all, if motivated, draw, paint, dance, sing, act and make innumerable artistic efforts without any guidance, but eventually and inevitably if we are to gain fulfilment from our efforts we will want and demand more help and expertise to perfect the intentions of our artistic expressions. We need to explore and discover the unique language which is inherent within every art form.

Using space

The ability to find space is in fact a skill that can be learned. The luxury of being the only one in a dance space is something we rarely enjoy and something children learning to dance rarely experience. It is necessary from the earliest age, or any age for that matter, to be able to find enough space in which to work adequately, taking into account the type and nature of the dance space and its surroundings, as well as the number of people occupying it. The need is so important and yet it is so often overlooked. It is very often assumed that the ability to find space happens naturally and every time. It does not. It needs to be learned and internalised and can, therefore, be taught. Once brought to the attention of the young dancer, and this can be done in a fun way, it is easily mastered. Unfortunately, it can just as easily be forgotten and so has to be continually repeated, reiterated in all sorts of ways to reinforce understanding. The best way not to forget is to eventually put it to use, consciously, in every session. A word of warning and advice, do not use the words 'spread out'. They do not have the same meaning as 'find space'.

Trust

Trust is another basic, but not exclusive element, of dance activity. It also takes time and repetition to achieve. Here, we are not only talking about confidence and security with the teacher, but in the dancers themselves and in relationship to each other. After all, it is they who will throw themselves and others around, it is they who will lift and climb and fall. It is too simplistic to suggest that the seeds of trust are sown in routine games; that is the dimension of drama. Trust for a dancer is fundamentally secured by a clear understanding of the nature of tension and relaxation. Very physical games playing with tension and relaxation can be created to allow children to play with trust in complete safety. The transition from understanding what each does, to using them with each other happens perfectly naturally. But, such an event as an end has to be carefully nurtured. In the final analysis tension allows dancers to lift safely.

They can only do this with each other so only routine and progressive work on this aspect will build up the required confidences. Relaxation allows the dancer to fall safely. This they do individually even though they may be part of a group, and so part of the routine of any dance session needs to be the development of courage.

Fear

Coming to terms with and learning to handle fear is not something many people have thought of as being fundamental to a dance activity. It is a known fact that babies survive accidents in which adults are seriously injured. There has to be a reason for this. It is more than likely to do with the differing levels of tension and relaxation, but these are controlled by emotional as well as intellectual states. In the instant before an accident the overriding emotion of fear causes tension, and the result is inevitable. However, a baby, in its innocence, knows no fear and is consequently in a state of some relaxation, thus injuries can be slight or even non-existent. Such an ability to put relaxation and tension to use in understanding or overcoming fear, is a powerful weapon in the armoury of skill needed by any moving person intent on dance activity. The need to be able to throw the body around without incurring injury holds excitement, stimulation, and should be desirable. If a teacher can achieve such a state in children, then the benefits are enormous; not just in terms of developing courage, which if unleashed in an unabated form is dangerous, but in understanding the relationship of the dancer to the floor. The willingness to try and fail, and to come to terms with that failure and to try again, is fostered, and the floor gradually becomes an aid – an extension of the body. The floor must be mastered and the way to do this is through teaching children how to fall – in the first place in a controlled and completely safe way, through understanding what the body actually does when it goes into a state of collapse. Such work begins on, or almost on, the floor and as mastery is gained the distance between the dancer and the floor is increased.

Structure and shape

Any dance session has a routine shape. Warm-up into learning experience into presenting what has been achieved; technique into improvisation into performance; beginning into middle into end. There are many ways of describing the cycle, but a cycle it is, safe and secure, controlled and disciplined, and only rarely are there genuine exceptions to the rule.

Recognise the rule and you are entitled to break it! Regardless of following the rule, or breaking it, a good dance lesson is about routine planning and preparation, density and intensity of movement experience, and ensuring that the lasting impression on both body and mind is that of being dance active.

The language

The art of dance has its own language – an expressive, communicative language. It's a language without words; it's body talk! But, what is the body language? How much technical ability is required? How many years of education and training are necessary for a person to build up a body language which can communicate with others?

The body talks from birth onwards, and thus it is safe to assume that we are all born with a language beyond words. The baby reaches out towards an adult to express his needs and to gain attention; the young child stamps his foot in anger and jumps for joy. Adults are less demonstrative in their use of body language, but posture and gesture usually reveal the mood of the moment.

If movement is the language then there is no language without a vocabulary. This vocabulary of movement has to be systematically built up. Technique contributes to the language but exploration of the individual's movement capability is the only way of achieving ownership of the language. Learning the movement of others is part of the exploration process but as a contributor rather than an initiator. Developing the ability to find the most articulate movement to express the intention is of paramount importance.

The dance relies on body talk as a means of expression and communication. It starts with known, familiar activities such as bending, stretching, twisting, turning, rising, falling, travelling, pausing, jumping, leaping and balancing. Through improvisation these body actions are enriched and developed by contrasts in their spatial and dynamic qualities. In other words, by changing the speed, strength, flow, dimension, direction, pathway and travel of the action a sequence of movement can be achieved which in turn can become a dance phrase.

The way the dancer uses space and dynamics influences the intention of the dance. In a sense they are the intonation of the language with movement actions being the words. Thus, the maker of dances must always be aware of where and how the action is taking place. A further consideration should be the relationship which the dancers have with the movement, other dancers and those observing the dance (the audience). After all, the dancer's body language is designed to communicate and relate with and to others, and this can only be achieved by paying special attention to the relationship possibilities available within each and every dance idea.

Trial and error is crucial to all of these exploratory activities. Making mistakes needs to be accepted as an ordinary and normal part of the process. In fact it is vital to the act of discovery and the creation of excitement which causes motivation, leading in turn to invention and innovation. Of course, it is impossible to separate body language into different categories because all dance contains all components of the language. It is, however, for learning and teaching purposes, possible to put the emphasis on one aspect without the exclusion of all the others. The language of dance is not something that can be separated from its other inherent knowledges and skills.

The analogy of travelling along a road as a means of understanding how the language of dance is acquired is a poor one, because the learning processes are not just linear. The analogy of building blocks is better because it allows for the simultaneous and sequential, but even this is not enough. Perhaps the analogy of a three dimensional jigsaw puzzle is the nearest – so long as its boundaries are infinite!

The method

Improvisation is the most potent means of exploration available to the dancer and the choreographer. It is the only way by which new movements can be found, and is fundamental to establishing a movement vocabulary. Both dancer and teacher can play with shape, space, dynamics, pattern, rhythm and the myriad of inter- and intra-relationship possibilities. It is the means by which we explore, are curious, can search, take risk, are inventive, may select, develop awareness, become sensitised and ultimately communicate. There are no secrets to offer as to how we get others to improvise; only quality stimuli and the confidence to do it.

Improvisation is about discovering possibilities; achieving surprise; finding the unpredictable. It is a period of finding out – of establishing basic movement material on which to begin building. This can be done alone and/or in groups. However, people do not simply improvise on command, and dancers, especially young ones, do not easily shed inhibitions. The teacher must actively show how easy it is to begin movement exploration from a dance idea, and this is only possible by 'doing'. No amount of thinking will bring it about – in fact, thought can be the very process that stifles or inhibits. Movement needs to be felt not thought about in the first place and it is the first stage of establishing honesty of expression and integrity of purpose. The teacher can only show by demonstration. He/she cannot improvise for the young dancer – they must do this for themselves. Gentle (or even harsh) verbal persuasion may be needed to nurture dancers into the nature, use and value of improvising. Ideas which immediately give rise to the potential for movement are essential. There is no better additional aid to a teacher's skill.

Improvisation is a tool for finding movement which accurately expresses a dance idea. Any old movement will not do. The first improvisational sweep may produce movement material which broadly expresses the idea, and with this as a base, refinement through further improvisation should bring about accurate expression and clarity of statement. Complexity can also be achieved by the refinement process and the reverse, of course, is also true. Early improvisation can produce too much movement. Selection must occur in further improvisation to achieve movement phrases and sequences that are direct and communicate with ease. Simplicity is the key.

The result

The combination of routine, language, and method will eventually result in the composition of a dance. To compose means to choreograph. Dances do not in reality take one minute, one hour or one day to create – they are usually, with respect to the few exceptions, the result of endless exploration, experimentation, heartache, improvisation, refinement, repetition and rejection. Making dances is no mean task, but the end results are often the most satisfying and gratifying moments ever experienced by the composer(s) of the dance. But, what makes a dance complete? Why do some dances create impact whilst others fail to appeal to artists and audience alike? Where can the composer of dances find the magic which makes the dance into an exciting, enigmatic art form?

The answer to these questions is not easy, but it has a lot to do with the creator of the dances – the choreographer. A choreographer, or a group of people involved in the composition (choreography) of dances must be aware of the traditional principles of composition, and should also know how to achieve, assess and encourage the very best quality of action.

There is no mystery in the word 'motif' when it is used in the context of making dances. A movement/dance motif is merely a pattern of activities and should be viewed in the same context as a musical phrase. Just as music usually needs several phrases to make up a piece, so a dance contains one or more motifs which are stated, developed and sometimes repeated. Most dance compositions need several motifs to create contrasts and to achieve that most elusive choreographic quality – surprise. The terminology of choreographic form may be similar or the same as that used in musical compositions, probably because historically music and dance were linked together. It must, however, be stated that just as music can flourish without dance, so too can dances be created without any musical accompaniment at all.

The dance, in common with all other arts, has to undergo a process of evolution from the first stimulus of an idea, through improvisation, and into a final form. This final form starts with the creation and development of movement motifs. These can range from the simple to the complex. Then, there are several accepted principles of dance composition/ choreographic form which exist in order to help the choreographer to organise the motifs into a completed dance form. They are necessary tools of the craft and should not be denied, nor should any person learning the craft be denied them. Young dancers have a right to know the rules. They cannot use them, ignore them and invent new ways unless this is so. Where ideas run dry they can be turned to as a stopgap, a device to achieve a temporary solution allowing the flow of creativity to continue. In any case, rules are a useful discipline; their very constraint is an advantage when the ground is unfamiliar. They contain the movement statement and stop the choreographer from rambling, and as an aid to conciseness they offer logic and encourage articulate expression. In a nutshell they act as foundation stones from which to start building.

The experimental can only be unique if the artist is aware of what is accepted and of what has gone before. In other words, before embarking on new and unfamiliar compositions be aware of the basic principles which have been tried and tested and are known to work. The best way of understanding the principles behind the composition of dance is through participation and involvement, exploration and experimentation, observation and assessment.

The beginnings of any and all art forms are creative and chaotic, and it is only adherence to self-discipline, selection and rejection, and to the principles which underpin the art form that completeness is achieved.

A dance idea could be a gesture, a rhythm, a word, a phrase, a piece of music, a prop, a personal experience, a colour, a cloud, a dream or almost anything. The stimulus, or starting point, must be a source of inspiration to the person, or persons, creating the dance as well as to those who are to dance it. A dance can be as short or as long as is required. It will be as short or as long as is needed to express the stimulus or dance idea. When searching for suitable ideas and stimuli it is very important to make sure that they have enough development possibilities.

Generally speaking, one dance session lasting approximately an hour will only cover a part of the whole dance idea. It is important to note that the dance ideas are not intended as complete sessions, nor do they set out to teach students stage by stage; you are the teacher and the initiator of the dance making process. So, do not rush! Spend time encouraging creativity and expression and be ready to stop and repeat so that you can clarify, acquire action of the very best quality from the dancers, and improve the overall quality of each stage of the dance activity before moving on.

All of the dance ideas offered in this book have been used successfully with boys and girls of different ages, from varied ethnic, cultural and class backgrounds, in schools, colleges and youth centres. They are only the tip of an ideas iceberg, yet are representative of a wealth of dance stimuli from known and original source material, which can be used according to differing needs, interests, abilities and expertise. They are intended to suggest, and not dictate, how a dance comes about. In one sense they are ordered and sequenced, for the purpose of indicating the importance of progression, but represent only possibilities within the area of dance education being taught. They are not particularly age- or stage-related but can be simplified or increased in difficulty according to desire or need. You are encouraged to take as little or as much advice as you need, and to develop the material in your own unique way.

Enough of suggestion and explanation. It is time to get up and to train, try out, explore, accept and reject the suggestions which are offered within the rest of this book. It is important to remember and to always keep in the forefront of your mind that you do not learn to dance or to make dances by sitting and studying. The dance is an exciting world of action, and it is only through trial and error on the dance floor that practice will perfect. The most mundane settings are often the places where the most creative and successful dance ideas are made.

Into action – the body

This section is concerned primarily with 'the body' and 'what the body can do'. It covers the following areas through a selection of varied and contrasting dance ideas:

Movement of the whole body

To show the body bending, stretching and twisting and to practise the familiar five basic body activities: travel, turn, elevation, gesture, weight transference.

Body parts

With a progression from basic 'loosening up' activities to the use of focus through body parts leading. Ideas include body parts leading, being in contact with each other and accompanying the action.

The body as a unit of motion and stillness

Stillness is by no means 'at rest' or 'relaxed', nor is it a passive state. It is a clear position with as much muscular awareness as action preceding it or proceeding from it.

Elevation

Skips, leaps and jumps are still dominant features of the most primitive, as well as the most skilfully contrived dances. To defeat gravity is a thrilling and gratifying experience to both the dancer and the dance audience. The ability to leap high in the air requires many hours of practice, but starts with the most simple of jumping and bouncing sequences.

Action words

Create a dance using the following ACTION words:

      travel   turn   open   close   fall   rise

Keep the sequence order, but explore different ways of performing them.

▶ Start with individual improvisations on a variety of ways of travelling, turning, opening, closing, falling and rising.

▶ Add changes of level and contrasting directions.

▶ Work in pairs moving with each other in unison (mirrors, shadows).

▶ Still in pairs, try moving one after the other as leader and follower, or as 'a conversation without words'.

▶ As a group, improvise on the idea of moving towards and away from each other, then – around, over, under, through and between.

2 Action sequence

▶ Improvise on bending, stretching and twisting. Develop from these explorations the use of opening, closing, rising and falling.

▶ Explore (exhaustively) ways in which the joints of the body can be used.

▶ Create a sequence using whole body actions. End the sequence with a jump or leap, followed immediately by stillness.

▶ Using the ideas of growing, revolving, and pulsating, create a dance sequence.

Here is a phrase/sequence of movement. Use it to create a dance.

> *Gesture leading into turn . . .*
> *Travel into balance . . .*
> *Tip, into transference of weight*
> *Stretch and rise . . .*
> *Travel and leap . . .*
> *Curl . . .*

▶ Choose one line (i.e. two activities) and experiment with the focus, direction, level, speed and weight of each action.

▶ Emphasise the transitions (changes) between each action, and spend time working on different transitions e.g. turning, shrinking, falling, rolling, growing etc.

▶ Experiment with balance and off balance.

▶ Finish the dance.

4 Sports day

Use sporting activities as the starting point for a dance based on the five basic body activities:

travel   turn   elevation   gesture   weight transference

Use changes in the speed and size of the action to create exaggeration and contrasts within the dance.

▶ Running, stopping and freezing in sports' shapes. Stress the need for sudden, clear statue shapes and quick changes in direction. The action words 'dodge', 'dart' and 'freeze' will improve the clarity and spacing.

▶ Develop each 'stopping and starting' phrase. Use each phrase to move from space to space as if really playing a sport – dodging, darting, hitting, throwing, or whatever. Make the movements larger than life – exaggerate them. At the end of each phrase freeze, in a clear statue shape 'as if someone's taken your photograph for a newspaper headline'.

▶ Try the above in slow motion – and teach the techniques of several other sports e.g. a tennis serve (reach, hit and run), putting the shot (spin, throw, stretch), a football goal (run and jump with head heading) etc.

▶ Put the sports day movements together to create the finished dance so that everybody is participating.

5 Obstacle race

▶ Compose dances in pairs with the emphasis on action and reaction.

▶ Create phrases of movement containing jumps, falls, rolls, stretches, twists and bends. See what spectacular endings can be found.

▶ Create a dance in pairs, threes, or fours based on the idea of an obstacle race.

Close eyes and/or turn out the lights and think about shadows, shapes and creatures.

▶ Improvise using the following action phrase: 'Slowly stepping, stopping, starting; rising, sinking, dodging, darting; leaping, meeting, slowly parting'. Try this alone, with a partner or as a group.

▶ Introduce a prop (such as a dustbin) for the dancer(s) to hide behind, move in and out of, creep around, between, and appear above and below it. Encourage the use of more props. Improvise with them one at a time.

▶ Develop a dance called 'Night Action'.

7 Beasts

▶ Improvise a group dance accompanied by evocative sounds to represent beasts meeting together. Contrast slow stepping with fast running; sudden leaping with slow sinking; turning and stopping; action and reaction.

▶ Leader and follower . . . relationships in pairs, group lines, group circles and formations. Change leaders frequently, in pairs and in lines. Use varied step patterns and ensure that the followers copy the leader exactly.

▶ Introduce the idea of cats as a stimulus for a dance using combinations of crouching, stretching, stalking, pouncing, and curling actions. Develop an action/reaction dance sequence between two squabbling cats.

8 Melodrama

An action packed dance using exaggeration and interaction of characters to create changes of mood.

▶ Make a 'composite sound tape' from sources such as the BBC's *Sound Effects for Silent Movies* and listen and discuss the musical changes within this composition. Then talk about the moods of mystery and suspense, panic, pathos, tension, heroic rescue, slapstick comedy and chaos which the music suggests.

▶ Organise the class into groups of three and allow time for discussion and decision about the story situation. Encourage clear exaggerated body actions and obvious changes in time, strength, level and relationship.

▶ Use the five basic body activities to improve and lengthen the action phrases within the dance.

▶ Let each group show its 'silent movie' sequence to the rest of the group to illustrate the need for clear starting and stopping shapes and a variety of the basic body activities, for thoughtful composition and for a careful build up to the climax of the dance.

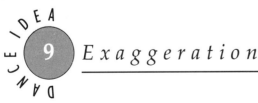

Exaggeration

Use exaggeration to explore a variety of caricatures such as 'workers' (e.g. window cleaner, road builder, househusband/wife) or 'baddies' (e.g bully, pickpocket, robber). Alternatively, explore tasks such as washing a car, decorating, preparing a meal.

▶ Improvise the sequence – check the accuracy of movement – refine it – all at normal size and speed.

▶ Experiment with moving the sequence faster then slower.

▶ Alter the size of the shape and movement to small then large.

▶ Combine the altered size and shape.

▶ Develop into pairs in unison, then fours in unison.

10 *Shifting weight*

Make a study where all the movement is caused by transferring weight alternately from on, to off balance. Improvise around the following:

▶ The spine divides the body into two parts. Using one side only whilst moving throws the body out of balance, i.e. off balance.

▶ Holding steady whilst extending and using our limbs causes us to have to concentrate on the distribution of our weight, i.e. on balance.

▶ Explore the sensation of 'off balance' through the following ideas: acrobats, tight-rope walkers, clowns, dreams.

▶ Work alone, then in pairs with one person initiating the weight transference into 'off balance' each time.

▶ Try transferring weight: on two or three body parts, for example from sitting, kneeling, lying and standing.

▶ Form transitions using travelling, turning, leaping and other whole body actions between each on and off balance shape.

▶ Use a box or a chair as a prop in the following way:
  – Sit and find a point of best balance.
  – Slowly move until you lose your point of balance.
  – Return to the balanced position in some different way.
  – Repeat from a standing position.
  – Add travelling, turning and/or jumping actions.
  – Develop in pairs and groups.

A short dance study based on stopping and balancing in numerous different ways.

▶ Work out phrases of running and stopping using some of the following 'stopping and balancing words':

wait	settle	freeze	wobble		collapse	hover
hold	perch	pause	stop	stay	linger	rest

▶ Work on each of the above actions separately, before combining them to create a dance.

▶ Emphasise the contrasts between speed, level, shape and strength, e.g. suddenly freezing or slowly settling; hovering high or collapsing low.

▶ Find different ways to travel using some of the 'travelling words' listed below. Try to combine an appropriate stopping action with your chosen method of travelling.

stamp	trot	creep	gallop	tiptoe
skip	stride	march	slither	scurry
run	walk	crawl	jump	slide	step

▶ Improvise using position, motion, pause.

Create a dance with one or more people based entirely on the use of the pause and the quality of stillness.

▶ Start by developing a feeling for stopping and starting through the following whole body activities: travelling, twisting, rising and falling, leaping, opening and closing.

▶ Focus on the contribution which each body part gives to the action, e.g. elbow, fingers and feet leading; chest rising; hips twisting. Experiment with other body parts leading either smoothly or jerkily.

▶ Improvise with the words 'stop . . . start . . . freeze . . . go . . . hold . . . continue . . . wait . . . arrive' and then form and perform your own list of 'stopping and starting' words.

- ▶ Find clear starting and stopping shapes using the idea of stillness, being in no way 'at rest' or 'relaxed'.

- ▶ Create: a series of quick, short movements separated by pauses; positions, each separated by motion. Experiment freely with timing and rhythmic changes.

- ▶ With the ideas of stillness and pause in mind, create a finished dance based on 'go to arrive/arrive to go'.

13 Movement and stillness

Using the following as inspiration:

Come to the edge
We might fall . . .
Come to the edge
It's too high!
Come to the edge
And they came . . .
And they flew!

▶ Create a sequence in threes or fives which contains all five basic body activities (travelling, turning, elevation, gesture, and weight transference). Emphasise the use of pause, stillness and balance.

▶ Work together using some of the material from the sequences to produce a finished dance.

14 *Body parts – loosening up*

With either the teacher or a member of the group as leader, create together a sequence of rhythmic shaking and loosening of body parts.

▶ Start with the group spaced out facing the leader, then shake the following body parts – hands, arms, feet, legs – to an 8 count, e.g. with the right arm:

shake right –2–3–4–5–6–7–8
shake left –2–3–4–5–6–7–8
repeat –2–3–4–5–6–7–8
etc.

Finish with a final stretch and contrast this tension with the rhythmic, relaxed quality of the shaking.

▶ Create similar sequences using other body parts, e.g. head, elbows, hands and feet.

▶ Organise the group in pairs facing each other and ask them to mirror the sequence, i.e. one shakes right as the other shakes left etc.

▶ Repeat the sequence in pairs, standing side by side, with the emphasis on coordinating the actions, i.e. moving in the same way at the same time.

Imagine that different body parts have been magnetised so that they pull together in the same way that magnetic poles are attracted; or that they resist and push away from each other, just as magnetic poles are repelled. Use the following suggestions to create a magnetic dance.

▶ Start with hands facing, but stretched as far away as they can reach. Then push hands together slowly and strongly as if they do not want to meet and are trying to resist each other as hard as they can. Lastly release, and with the release from the magnetic force, try stretching or turning, running, jumping or falling.

▶ Work on other parts of the body being magnetised too, e.g. a hand might be attracted to a knee, an elbow to hip, a foot to hand or maybe even a foot to the head! Emphasise the tension between body parts as they meet and part.

▶ In pairs, explore the following possible combinations:

foot to hand
hand to hand
elbow to knee
back to back
side to side

Start alone and gradually (through tension and resistance) meet and part. Use 'releases' from the magnetic force (jumping stretching, spinning, spiralling, running, falling) to create contrasts in the speed, strength, level, and shape of activity.

▶ Look at examples from the group, then observe magnetism (tension) and release (relaxation). Comment on the differences between closed and open body shapes and on the changes in strength and speed.

▶ Use elastic to create tension and release. Attach the elastic to one wrist and the opposite ankle, and experiment with twisting, turning, stretching and shrinking actions. Then, alone, in pairs, or in threes, use different body parts and explore the 'magnetic' idea using elastic.

16 *Body parts leading*

Movement begins to be articulate when certain parts of the body take the major role . . . as when parts of an orchestra are heard above the others.
(From *A Handbook for Modern Educational Dance* by Valerie Preston.)

Each limb can take a solo part, i.e. the four quarters of the body 'singing' one after the other.

Explore the above statements through the following tasks:

▶ Create a fairly slow dance when surfaces of the arms lead the movement using twisting, gathering and reaching actions along straight and curved pathways.

▶ Create a quicker dance where joints of the legs lead, and gestures and jumps are used.

▶ Create a sequence led by the chest where rising movements are contrasted with deeper movement led by the pelvis. Remember that the torso can lead the body into twists, contractions, elevations and stretches.

Body parts can touch, and body parts can make sound. Contact can be audible or tactile. Two parts of the body can be near one other, gently touch, interlink, surround one another.

Improvise the following:

▶ Body parts going away from, avoiding, and going around each other.

▶ Both parts can be equally active, or one part can dominate. In fact, one part of the body can carry on a conversation with another part as if two people were talking.

▶ Body parts striking each other in such a way as to cause sound, e.g. slap, clap, stamp. Use body parts in contact with the floor to create sound.

▶ Explore both ideas with a partner.

▶ Create a finished dance with a partner where movement is caused by touch and where touch creates sound.

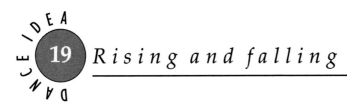

18 Voice dance

Body activities and moving body parts can cause and be accompanied by sound made by the voice.

▶ Experiment with different types of movement and find the appropriate sounds to go with these movements.

▶ Improvise a sequence of movement. As it becomes refined, punctuate the movement with appropriate sound.

▶ With a partner, put the two solo pieces together as a duet. Adapt the movement and sound accordingly to develop the relationship that evolves.

Sound can, of course, generate movement. Try the two following ideas, first by improvising and then eventually by setting the movement and sound so that a finished dance results.

▶ Clap a rhythmic phrase. Create several movement phrases that mirror or even ride over the sound. As the dance becomes fixed, perform some of the phrases with the clapping, and others without. Alternatively allow another dancer to be the source of the clapping.

▶ Using your voice, spell out your name, using each letter to change and develop the sequence and style of the dance.

19 Rising and falling

Elevation does not just mean jumping and leaping in a variety of ways. It also means understanding how to rise up from the floor and fall down to the ground in as many different ways as possible.

▶ Improvise with rising and falling movements. Try all the movements slowly. Try all the movements quickly. Mix according to the natural flow of the movement.

▶ Work with a partner on the idea of 'reaching over and getting under'. Under no circumstances touch each other.

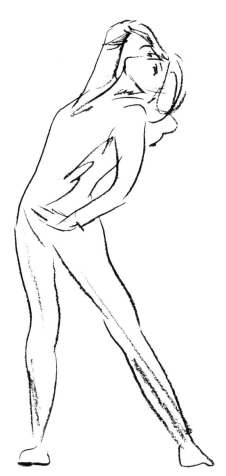

▶ Work with another partner on the idea of 'getting over and getting under'. This idea should allow you to dive over, roll under, climb on each other, crawl through and so on.

▶ Take the really good ideas from your work and create a dance where there is an occasional jump but where the emphasis is on nearly, but not quite, leaving the floor – in other words 'rising to fall and falling to rise'.

20 Bounce, spring, explode

Jumping and leaping is enjoyable. It can be exhausting. Energy needs to be used efficiently otherwise control is lost or the jump/leap hardly gets into the air. Jumps and leaps also express mood and character and should be explored emotionally as well as technically. Remember – landing is part of jumping and needs as much concentration and attention.

Using improvisation as the source of the movement explore thoroughly the type of jump brought about by each of the following.

▶ Bouncing – change shape whilst bouncing.

▶ Springing – change shape whilst springing.

▶ Exploding – change shape one jump at a time.

    Deal with each separately to begin with. Ensure you understand what the type of jump brought about 'feels' like.

▶ Create a movement sequence where bouncing, springing and exploding jumps and leaps dominate the action.

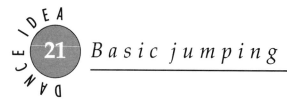

21 Basic jumping

There are five basic jumps:

▶ From one foot to the same foot.

▶ From one foot to the other foot.

▶ From one foot to both feet.

▶ From both feet to both feet.

▶ From both feet to one foot.

Create a sequence using all five jumps, not just once but a number of times. Vary the order. Be as inventive as you can.

22 Flight

Take the following words:

> fly   soar   swirl   whirl   glide

▶ Improvise movements using these words ensuring that the emphasis is on elevation and leaving the floor.

▶ Pick the best of your improvised ideas and set them as a short solo piece.

▶ Take three of these solos and play with them until a trio dance is established.

▶ Put two trios together so that the study in elevation becomes a small group dance for six people.

▶ Go back to the six individual solos, inter-relate them in the space but keep them separate, do not attempt to establish any relationship with other dancers, immediately move into the two trio pieces, immediately move into the finish with the dance for six.

▶ Call the dance 'Birds in flight'.

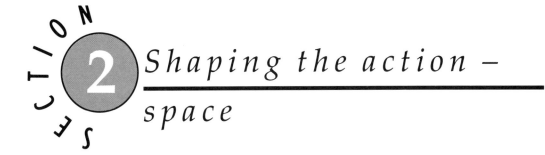

2 *Shaping the action –*

space

This section is primarily concerned with 'space' and 'where the body can go'.   It covers the following areas through a variety of ideas:

Shapes and sizes

There are only four basic shapes that we can make with our bodies – the rest are all variations. The four basic body shapes arise out of the simple fact that the body can bend, stretch, and twist.

By stretching in a linear fashion, the body pierces through the space. This shape can pierce any one of the spatial areas, and is arrow-like in shape.

The body may stretch and spread at the same time and in this way will form a two-dimensional flat shape and is wall-like in shape.

When the body bends, the spine curves and a rounded ball-like shape emerges.

If the body twists at any point, then a three-dimensional screw-like shape is formed.

Thus the four basic body shapes are:

arrow,   wall,   ball,   screw

and these shapes can be made to travel, leap, turn, contract, expand and freeze.

The size of movement is also important to allow the dancer to perform at, and with, varying degrees of extension and contraction.

Spatial areas – levels, directions, dimensions, diagonals

The most simple and easily understood spatial areas are the three levels of movement – high, medium and deep. The high level is bordered by the ceiling, the deep level by the floor and the medium level is bordered by walls. The four facets of the medium level are:

in front
behind
to the right
to the left

The following spatial concepts can and will arise out of improvisations using different levels:

above – below
over – under
out of – into

The use of space will be further improved by stressing direction and dimension. The main directions are based on the principle of the three dimensions – height, width and depth. These are symbolised by three lines intersecting at the body centre, giving rise to spatial concepts of:

forwards – backwards
side – side
up – down

Pathways through the space can be direct or indirect along straight or curved lines.

The three levels connect the three dimensions which in turn offer six directions that also include three planes and four diagonals. Experimenting with movement contained within any of these areas, and/or connecting them, results in movements which open and close; rise and fall; advance and retreat; wheel and turn; twist and spin; revolve and spiral; and tip and balance.

The space around a dancer is divided into two categories: 'personal space' which can be thought of as a huge balloon which extends as far as the body can reach without moving off the spot, and 'general space' which involves the whole room area.

Personal space – the kinesphere

When in stance, and the limbs are extended into space, points are reached beyond which further extension is impossible. Connect all of these points and you create the kinesphere in which you may fully extend or contract. The kinesphere is constantly re-created when the dancer changes position i.e. it is carried around with the dancer.

Activities within the personal sphere of movement are very much concerned with contraction and extension of the body and body parts. They involve gestures with legs and arms, floor and air patterns, turning and twisting, rising and falling.

Movements may either go outwards from the centre of the body, back to the centre of the body, or may travel peripherally around the outside linking directional, dimensional and diagonal points.

Movements involving the centre mean use of the whole body. These movements are intensive, charged with vitality, repellent and impellent. They penetrate the space. On the other hand, those led from point to point on the periphery of the kinesphere involve limbs only and are sometimes seen as cold and impassive. Peripheral transitions fill the space and sweep around, surrounding our own personal space.

General space – orientation

Weight transference, pathways, travelling and elevation take the dancer and his/her kinesphere beyond the spot and bring them into contact with the wider area of general space.

From the outset both teacher and dancer will be concerned with orientation in space and this involves awareness of position in general space, and a clear conception of focus and direction.

23 *From shape to shape*

▶ Improvise using a variety of ways of changing from one body shape to another, e.g. by stretching, curling, twisting, jumping, rolling, stepping and so on.

▶ Create shapes which stay on/or around the spot and transitions which travel into a new space.

▶ Move quickly or slowly; strongly or lightly; at high, low and medium levels.

▶ Work in groups to create a dance consisting entirely of unusual movement.

24 *Shadow shapes*

▶ In pairs, create body shapes with the emphasis on exact mirror images.

▶ Explore changes (transitions) between the shapes, e.g. unfolding from the centre of the body into wide/stretched and thin/narrow shapes; twisting and turning into curved/rounded and screwed-up shapes.

▶ Try a variety of relationship possibilities, e.g. facing each other; side by side; one behind the other.

► *Shadow, shadow curled up small,*
  I can make you grow up tall,
  Now we're stretching high and wide,
  Shadow, shadow's at my side.
  Turning, twisting round and round –
  Shadow's rolling on the ground.
  Run away, shadow go!
  I can't lose my shadows though!?!

► Use the poem as a source of movement ideas and create a duet based on shadows.

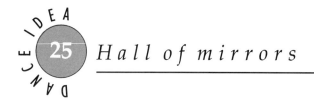

Hall of mirrors

Take a trip through a hall of mirrors – the kind you see at a fairground. Explore the possibilities of this task to create numerous, humorous body shapes and to form a dance comedy.

▶ Start with the group facing the leader and mirroring a variety of 'odd' shapes – high, low, wide and twisted. Emphasise the fact that the slightest movement can lengthen and twist the arm, shorten and bend the legs, stretch and turn the neck, and so on.

▶ Improvise individually on a variety of transitions from shape to shape. Search for variety in shape – tall, wide, spiky, wobbly, short etc.

▶ Search for variety in the transitions between the shapes – stepping, turning, jumping, running, etc.

▶ Work in two large groups, with one group spaced out as the mirrors and the other group moving individually from mirror to mirror, using a combination of interesting pathways and transitions so that everyone has the opportunity to mirror and to be mirrored.

▶ Observe demonstrations of particularly effective 'comic' sequences by the class and discuss what makes them humorous.

Shapes alone and shapes together

Work in groups of four to create dance phrases and sequences based on the following statements:

'The arrow shape penetrates personal space and then shoots through general space along a direct pathway with a clear focal point.'

'The wall shape divides the space in front and behind the body with activities like stretching, swaying, stepping, leaping and cartwheeling.'

'Back-bends, somersaults and rolls are inherent in the ball shape.'

'The turns and twists which depict the screw shape can rise and fall whilst spiralling, spinning or wringing their way around the body.'

▶ Create a dance using the four basic body shapes of arrow, ball, screw, wall.

▶ As the dance takes shape, work on the interaction between shapes and pathways, e.g. the 'arrow' divides the 'wall' or pierces the rounded 'ball' shapes; the 'screw' twists and weaves its way in and out of the 'wall' and surrounds the 'ball' shape.

▶ Try working on each body shape as a group 'unit', and then interacting with other groups.

▶ Discuss other possible pathways (e.g. circle, spiral, zig-zag, figure of eight, loop) and explore the floor and air patterns associated with each one.

▶ Bring all the ideas together, finish the dance.

27 Levels and directions

In pairs, use the following words to demonstrate an understanding of changes in level and direction, e.g.

above – below
retreat – advance
through – around

▶ Improvise using different relationship possibilities, e.g. action and reaction, leader and follower, moving simultaneously, moving in turn.

▶ Experiment with changes in level, speed and direction i.e. high/low; fast/slow; forward/backwards/sideways.

▶ Introduce the idea of using 'props' e.g. hoops to move through, benches to balance on, equipment to clamber over, under, around and between.

▶ 'Agreement, meeting, conflict'. Create a sequence using these three words in relationship to different parts of the body, showing awareness of the three main spatial areas.

28 Space and flow

In pairs, use contrasts in the direction and flow of action to create a series of question and answer phrases based on:

▶ Flexible actions using free flow followed by direct movements using bound flow.

▶ Direct movements using bound flow followed by flexible actions using free flow.

▶ Through improvisation discover how your body naturally uses the elements of space and flow. Consider the following during your explorations:

SPACE QUALITIES
(*i*) Direct – straight, keeping strictly to the path, attention kept directly on the place of arrival.
(*ii*) Flexible – roundabout, wavy, undulating, generous in use of space, several parts of the body going into different places at the same time.

FLOW QUALITIES
(*i*) Free – in a movement action where it is difficult to stop, the flow is fluent or 'free'.
(*ii*) Bound – in a movement action capable of being stopped or held without difficulty at any moment, the flow is restricted or 'bound'.

▶ Allow the improvisation to set itself into a fixed sequence where the two space qualities and the two flow qualities are clearly articulated. Ensure there is contrast in level, direction and dimension.

29 Symmetry and asymmetry

Body shapes are symmetric when the limbs produce shapes that are identical either side of the spine. If the body shapes produced either side of the spine are very different then they are described as asymmetric. Asymmetric shapes often cause imbalance and so the body tips over and begins to travel. Symmetrical shapes tend to cause pause or stillness and so are virtually static. However, it is possible for the balanced shapes of symmetry to move and the imbalanced shapes of asymmetry to remain still.

▶ Improvise, alone, creating different body shapes where the limbs are identical in shape either side of the spine. These shapes can be on high, medium or low levels.

▶ Now find ways of connecting half a dozen of these symmetrical shapes by disturbing one side of a shape, causing movement, pathway, travel, and bring it to stillness by reforming into the next symmetrical shape.

▶ In small groups of fours, fives, sixes and sevens experiment with creating group shapes that are symmetrical.

▶ Agree on six interesting symmetrical shapes. The symmetrical shapes will cause you to come together to form them. Break up the shape by the use of asymmetry, thus dispersing the group. Reform into the next symmetrical shape, and so on.

▶ Let dancers in the group improvise their own asymmetrical shapes and pathways between the group shapes.

▶ Work out different changes between each of the symmetrical shapes, but all the dancers must learn them exactly and these transitions should be performed in unison.

▶ Either alone, with a partner, or in small groups, create a dance based on different types of step and gesture, where ideas of symmetry and asymmetry are important.

 **30** *The journey*

Use your knowledge of different spatial areas, focus and projection from personal into general space to create a dance depicting the strength and hardship suffered by refugees who have to leave their homeland to make a new life for themselves elsewhere. Use dance to describe their long hazardous journey.

▶ Start apart from each other, then gradually through eye contact or touch, slowly step together. In other words, allow time for the individuals to express their identity before becoming one of the group.

▶ Introduce the idea of travelling towards a focal point and emphasise looking back at the homeland left behind as well as looking forward with hope to the new 'promised land'.

▶ Use different directions and levels to improvise on the following 'possible progressions':

crossing rivers, climbing twisted pathways, balancing across narrow bridges etc. Use a variety of relationships e.g. individual and group, pairs and trios, small and large groups.

▶ Experiment with a variety of line, group and circle formations with shrinking, growing and swaying actions.

▶ In groups of three, explore different ways of getting over, under, around and through human obstacles. Use different body parts, levels and relationship situations to form human barriers.

▶ Choreograph a dance in which some small groups create barriers and obstacles for other groups to overcome in various ways. Introduce 'props' such as a long piece of material to create a flowing river, elastic to create a tangled web, hoops to move through and around.

Patterns in the air, patterns on

the floor

31

Whatever the arms do the legs will echo. Whatever the legs do the arms will follow. Arm movements occur mostly in the air and leg movements occur largely on the floor. Movements of the arms describe patterns in the air and movements of the legs cause patterns on the floor. Air patterns follow floor patterns and vice versa. It is impossible for the arms to move in curves and the legs to move angularly at one and the same time. Try it and see!

▶ Move continuously in soft, curved lines, relating all body parts to curved motion.

▶ On the spot, experiment with angular movement of arms and legs.

▶ Think about lyrical and dynamic phrasing. Create some such phrases, but each time a new phrase is begun, clearly change direction.

▶ With a partner, create a dance demonstrating that you understand the difference between clarity of movement and confusion of movement.

▶ In small groups create a dance on the following idea: 'Creatures of the air; Creatures of the earth'.

On the spot and into space

32

Improvise on the following idea:

▶ Contrast travelling with combinations of movements on the spot.

▶ Try the idea again but emphasise the importance of changing levels.

▶ Develop a three-part solo dance in which:

Part one contains extensive projection of movement from a stationary position into space.

Part two consists of movement from the stationary base to an area some three metres away.

Part three uses extensive projection outward into space by actually travelling through space.

▶ Experiment with position and pathways and put three of these solo pieces together to create a trio dance. Make the appropriate body, spatial, and inter-personal relationship adjustments.

33 Lines, pathways and pattern

Straight lines, curved lines, long lines, short lines, thick lines, thin lines, horizontal, vertical, parallel, diagonal, spiral and zig-zag – all sorts of lines.

▶ Take the line ideas that allow for solo work and improvise shapes and pathways.

▶ Take the line ideas that need a group to form them and create a short dance based on pathways and pattern.

▶ Seek out the painting by Paul Klee called *Snake Paths*. Create a dance together using ideas from the painting.

34 Ritual and mourning

▶ Play a ritual drumbeat to accompany stepping in lines and circles as in a procession. Introduce opening/closing, swaying and turning actions to represent togetherness; then provide a focal point which each member of the group reaches towards one by one.

▶ Work without accompaniment on three or four 'motifs' based on bowing and uplifting, lifting and reaching, lowering and crouching, opening, closing and turning, involving moving in unison, leading/following, one at a time, and in canon.

▶ Every culture has its own way of mourning its dead. Traditionally it is a time for people to come together to share their grief. To represent this togetherness, work as one large group in a circle (with centre circle as focal point) or in line formation (with a high diagonal focal point). Share ideas and build up a ceremonial dance made up of slow, step patterns, clear body shapes and exaggerated gestures.

▶ Choose ritualistic pieces of music with regular rhythms from several cultures – South America, India, China, Africa. Talk about the differences in spiritual expression between them and create dances based on them.

Colouring the action – dynamics

In this section the dynamic qualities of dance are highlighted. The emphasis is on 'how' the body moves. It covers the following through varied ideas:

Dynamic contrasts

Dealing with accepted factors causing qualities of motion, separately and in combination, together with dramatically inspired contrasts.

Rhythm

Including exploration into metric and non-metric possibilities as well as the use of sounds, words, live and recorded music.

35 Weight and time

▶ Compose two contrasting movement phrases consisting of:

– strong percussive actions followed by strong, sustained recoveries; and

– strong, sustained actions followed by strong, percussive recoveries.

▶ Use the phrases above to create an 'action/reaction' dance.

▶ Investigate the dynamic qualities of other contrasting movement phrases, e.g. light, percussive actions followed by light, sustained recoveries, and in reverse, light, sustained actions followed by light, percussive recoveries.

▶ Emphasise the contrasts between different weight/time combinations by introducing difference dynamic words and phrases e.g.

Strong/sudden . . . explode, punch, whip.
Light/sudden . . . dart, dash, flicker.
Strong/sustained . . . press, wring and pull.
Light/sustained . . . glide, float and smooth.

▶ Create a solo dance from the phrase 'Pow-zowie-wham! Here's BATMAN' demonstrating contrasts in weight (strong/light) and time (sudden/sustained).

36 Words and whispers

Words can be used to create continuity or interrupt the flow of movement. They also have other inherent dynamic qualities. There are:

slow words e.g. creep, crawl, slither, linger, melt:

quick words e.g. dart, dab, sparkle, flicker, flutter, shiver;

light words e.g. glide, float, swivel, whirl, hover;

strong words e.g. push, pull, twist, stamp, whip.

Select words from those listed above to describe the different ways in which animals/insects move.

▶ Improvise on at least two words, and a maximum of five, to form dynamic action phrases e.g.

Swooping – swirling – sinking and sliding.
Darting – darting, slowly sinking – leap and twirl away.
Jumping here – jumping there – jumping, jumping everywhere.
Freeze – crumple – Freeze – crumple to the floor.
Curling – writhing – twisting and unfolding.
Expand – contract – explode – cascade.
Round and round – up and down – sink and roll away.
Crouches – stretches – darts.
Sparkle – spatter – shoot and swirl.

37 Dynamic actions – easy

All movement actions, whether functional or artistic, are based on eight fundamental units . . . called effort actions.
(From *A Handbook for Modern Educational Dance* by Valerie Preston.)

After exploring the following tasks, is this statement true or false?

▶ Take the eight effort action words: thrust – float; slash – glide; wring – dab; press – flick, and create a very short phrase of movement using each effort action word in an expressive sense. Do not think, simply respond in terms of what the word means to you.

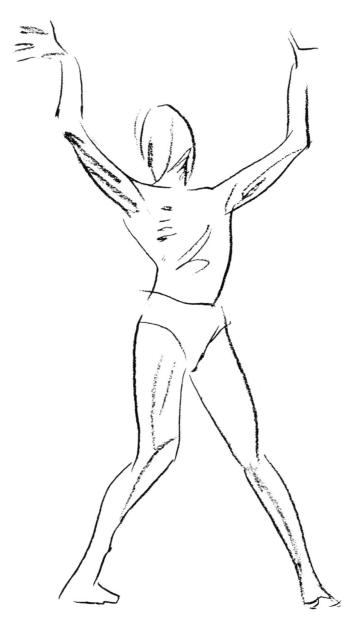

► Analyse each effort action in terms of its component parts and practise the type of movement they produce.

Firm – sudden – direct	*THRUST*
Fine – sustained – flexible	*FLOAT*
Firm – sudden – flexible	*SLASH*
Fine – sustained – direct	*GLIDE*
Firm – sustained – flexible	*WRING*
Fine – sudden – direct	*DAB*
Firm – sustained – direct	*PRESS*
Fine – sudden – flexible	*FLICK*

38 Dynamic actions – hard

▶ Construct a movement pattern, then

– perform it at normal speed, then
– move it twice as fast
– and twice as slow;

– perform it at normal speed again, then
– move it using as much space as possible
– and in a very restricted space;

– perform it at normal speed once more, then
– give it all the strength you can
– and finally with all the delicacy you can muster.

▶ Create a short dance mixing all of these possibilities.

▶ Now create a short dance using specific parts of the body to demonstrate the full variety of effort actions.

▶ Experiment with effort actions that have completely opposite dynamic qualities. Note the abrupt changes they cause in movement.

▶ In pairs, create a dance using clear dynamic elements and actions accompanied by voice sounds.

▶ From the duet work, put three duos together and complete the dance in a group.

39 Dynamic phrase – simple

Individually create a short pathway. Other dancers should be avoided. Re-adjust the length and timing of the pathway until it can be travelled uninterrupted from beginning to end, regardless of how many other dancers cross or come close. Practise the pathway over and over until its length, beginning and ending are sure. The pathway can either be straight or curved.

▶ Anywhere in the pathway add the following, strictly in order: a jump or leap, a turn, and a gesture.

▶ At the beginning create a still shape as a 'start' shape.

- ▶ After the last movement, be it jump, turn, or gesture, transfer the weight by any means other than the feet.
- ▶ Finish in a balanced shape – but not on your feet.
- ▶ Perform the dynamic phrase.

40 Dynamic phrase – complex

Walking to a steady beat of twelve counts, establish a straight or curved pathway.

- ▶ Somewhere on the pathway set a movement that lasts three counts.
- ▶ Add a low movement.
- ▶ A turn.
- ▶ An elevation.
- ▶ A movement diagonally backwards.
- ▶ An accent in two places.
- ▶ A movement diagonally upwards and forwards.
- ▶ A rhythmic pattern in the feet that is pronounced.

Each movement must be added in the order given and all movements need to be maintained regardless of new ones added.

- ▶ Give the phrase an unusual ending.

41 Rhythmic echoes

Create an echo dance with a partner.

- ▶ One dancer leads the other echoes. Emphasise the exact reproduction of timing, force (strength) and body activities.

► Echo exactly, one after the other, a strong rhythmic stepping phrase.

► A quick, strong jumping phrase followed by a series of slow, light turns.

► Work on forming three clear phrases of movement which include changes in level, direction and pathway as well as highlighting contrasting dynamics. Spend time repeating each phrase so that it can be reproduced exactly to form an echo.

► Give each pair two of the same percussion instruments with which to create their own short musical and accompanying movement phrases. Extend these into a dance in which each dancer takes a turn to lead and echo the actions, shape and level of his or her partner.

► Create echo dances in groups of four, but with changes in relationship, i.e. one leads, three echo; two lead, two echo; three lead, one echoes.

► Or echo by positioning:
  – one behind the other;
  – side by side;
  – facing each other;
  – apart from each other;
  – back to back. (etc.)

42 Storm dance

When the wind whirls, curls and swirls – WHOOSH
'Things' fly and fling and twirl – SWOOSH
Spiralling round and down and round – SSH
Floating and flying to the ground – WHEE
Then thunder cracks and rolls and crashes – BOOM
As lightening leaps and darts and flashes – CRACK
Raindrops drop upon the ground
Beating, bouncing, pattering sounds . . . T–T–T–
Soon the storm had died away – SSSH
It's left a rainbow on its way.

► Work in groups and use the poem to combine changing dynamic actions with voice sounds and words, and create a storm dance.

43 Talking feet

Create a dance based on a combination of rhythmic step patterns. Use the following rhyme to help the improvisations.

Listen, listen to the feet . . .
Big feet, small feet,
Strong feet, light feet,
Toes are tapping,
Feet are talking.

One foot, two foot, three foot, four . . .
Creeping creatures have some more.
Feet are dancing in a line . . .
It's crazy caterpillar time!

▶ Accompany this theme with both metric and non-metric sound sources. In other words, allow the dancers to interpret the words of the poem without any music at all and/or provide music to inspire and accompany the action.

▶ Organise the group into small groups and teach several different group formations, e.g. lines, circles, half circles, parallel lines, and diagonals etc. Ask each group to create and perform a skip pattern during which they leave and return to their starting position.

▶ Create a comedy dance based on a tap-dancing class with dancers moving in unison with you as their leader. Let the dancers create their own showpiece solo, pair and group routines within the dance.

44 Working rhythms

Create a group composition with a strong rhythmic quality based on traditional working actions.

▶ Improvise around different kinds of working actions, e.g. people in the countryside who worked on the land might have made up a harvesting dance which would include: strong, swinging, scything actions; scooping and gathering; carrying and stacking; pulling and pushing and so on.

► Increase the size and strength of each action, then use stepping, turning, rising and sinking to develop each working action into a rhythmic dance phrase.

► Organise the group into units of four and suggest moving in unison, one after the other and in pairs.

► Encourage regular, rythmic step patterns at high and low levels in forwards, backwards and sideways directions.

► Organise the class into three groups and give each group the same working motif. Stagger the start of each group and insist on regular repetition – thus, each group will be making the same actions but at different times.

► Create a 'whole group' dance with different groups performing related tasks at different times, e.g. digging, sowing, scything. Create a final working movement for the whole group to do in unison, e.g. passing bundles of hay or pushing forwards and pulling backward.

45 *Rhythmic improvisation*

Work without prior discussion or preparation on the following tasks:

► Clap a rhythmic phrase, then use it and variations on it to create a dance sequence.

► Create a duet with one person moving in metric rhythm, the other in non-metric. You may use any idea or theme for your motivation, e.g. machines, time, the seasons, life cycles, but there must be a relationship between you.

Select a series of contrasting musical phrases from a popular classical recording.

► Record each phrase twice. Listen to the phrase, then when it is repeated react spontaneously attempting to show in movement what the music suggests to you.

► Listen to the dynamic quality of each musical statement then repeat that quality in action.

► Create an 'echo' dance in pairs, in which the dancers take turns to make statements for their partners to echo. Use the recorded music at first, but then ask each pair to echo their actions unaccompanied.

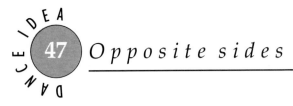

47 Opposite sides

A dramatic dance based on conflict and confrontation.

▶ Start by thinking (in movement terms) of opposites, such as: rival groups of people, day and night, fire and water, colours clashing.

▶ In pairs, improvise the build up of tension and suspense through stepping and pausing, turning and pausing, advancing and retreating and changes of level. Find ways of building up tension and suspense – two against two – with slow, rhythmic stepping towards and away from each other; pausing and staring.

▶ Work on showing what happens when the two sides meet, perhaps introducing jumps and turns and other sudden, strong actions. Try strong, slow pressing actions towards and away from each other using palms of hands, feet, knees and elbows, but ensure that the dancers do not make actual contact with each other.

▶ Choose one pair or group to perform its sequence as an illustration of clear changes in level, timing, body activities and relationship situations.

▶ Discuss the 'demonstration dance' with the class, and use it to improve the quality and performance of other pairs and groups.

▶ Use the 'prologue' from *West Side Story* to stimulate and develop the work into a finished dance.

48 Movement density

▶ Find and record a very, or relatively, simple piece of music.

▶ Improvise with it until the music is utterly familiar.

▶ Now, weave around it a dominant theme with as much detailed and complex movement as can be sustained.

49 Go Wind!

A dance idea based on the poem *Go Wind* by Lilian Moore.

Go wind, blow
Push wind, swoosh . . .
Shake things
Take things
Make things
Fly! . . .

Ring things
Swing things
Fling things
High . . .

Go wind, blow
Push things . . . whee . . .
No wind, no,
Not me
Not me!

▶ Select the action words from the poem – go, blow, push, swoosh, shake, fly, ring, swing, fling, push and whee – and concentrate on their dynamic qualities i.e. speed, strength, etc. Spend time working out ways to express the words in movement – introduce going and stopping, turning, leaping, circling and spiralling, falling and rolling actions. Improvise on each line of the poem, line by line. Accompany the words with voice sounds and enhance and improve the shape, size and quality of each action.

▶ Experiment with speaking and moving at the same time.

▶ Perform the dance using voice sounds only.

50 Questions and answers

Play percussion and/or use live or recorded music to demonstrate a series of question and answer phrases. Interpret these in movement illuminating the changes in dynamic qualities.

▶ Create action/reaction phrases to a variety of musical questions and answers.

▶ Allow time for the dancers to listen to, then work on the contrasts, in each question and answer phrase. Suggest using a variety of levels, body parts and body activities to reinforce the changes in speed, strength and flow.

▶ Try working in pairs with one person asking the questions and the other giving the answers.

▶ Work in pairs without any accompaniment, creating new/original question and answer phrases.

▶ Each pair selects contrasting percussion instruments, e.g drum and bells, block and shaker and then creates question and answer dance phrases moving in time to their own percussion.

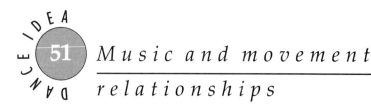

Music and movement
relationships

Do the following three tasks solo and separately.

▶ Choose a single piece of music in a style other than 'chart' music.

▶ Improvise a number of times moving in direct response, imitating the rhythm exactly/directly.

▶ Improvise a number of times moving in direct opposition to the rhythm.

▶ Decide on the mood or theme of the music. Improvise responding only to the mood or theme. Disregard the phrasing or dynamics of the music, using it only as background.

▶ With a partner, create a finished duet on one of these three ideas.

▶ Take a duet from each of the three ideas. Do not change the duets at all. Put them together in the same space. See what happens.

▶ Finally re-adjust only the pathways and placements until movement relationships are established and the dance, for six, works.

Colour contrasts

A rainbow is sometimes used to symbolise harmony. Taken separately, each colour has its own character and can suggest different moods to different people.

▶ Individually explore the mood and expression of colours of your own choice.

▶ Improvise in pairs and small groups around the idea of colours clashing.

▶ In three groups, create a dance in four sections i.e. cool colours, fiery colours, sombre colours and the rainbow. Each group takes responsibility for a section before joining together for the last section.

COOL COLOURS

The first section of the dance is inspired by the cool colours – the silvers, the blues and the greens; the colours of the grass, the sea and the sky. Use slow, light, lyrical qualities to combine opening, closing, turning, spiralling, rising and falling.

FIERY COLOURS

A combination of golds, reds, oranges and yellows. Try out a variety of quick/strong and quick/light qualities with darting, exploding, flickering, growing and shrinking actions using a variety of body shapes and body parts.

SOMBRE COLOURS

Representing black, dark blues, purples, greys and dark browns. Use strong/slow dynamic qualities and advancing, retreating and surrounding actions.

THE RAINBOW

A final section in which the three colour groups meet and interact with each other. Use the movement, phrases and sequences previously created, and finish the dance in a 'rainbow' as a symbol of colour harmony.

4 *Making the action –*

choreography

This last section is not only concerned with what the body can do, where it can go, and how it moves, but especially with 'From what and how a dance is composed.' The principles of composing, performing and appreciating apply for each idea and are assumed to be understood. Using a variety of possibilities it covers the following areas:

Motifs

To show the ease with which a motif is developed and repeated from an improvised sequence of movement, and to establish it as a pattern of activity that expresses and communicates the dance idea.

Choreographic directions

Becoming familiar with the universally accepted pathways, patterns and formations that are possible when dancers move together.

Choreographic form

Considering the commonly accepted structures of binary, ternary, rondo, canon, and theme and variation/contrast/development as the basic tools of organising a dance.

Choreographic ideas

Hopefully stimulating and inspirational. Capable of being interpreted differently in form and content, giving rise to breaking down established rules and demonstrating the infinite variation possible. Very little or no explanation is offered – imagination and vision are the key to their development and potential.

It is important when searching for, coming across, and eventually choosing a dance idea to ensure that the stimuli is rich in movement potential. An idea should contain scope for the development of body awareness, space, dynamics, relationships and form. There are important aspects to development that should be noted, such as the logical progression inherent to the forwarding of any dance idea, improvisation into set motifs and their variation and repetition, phrases and sequences forming directions and patterns, structure or form that clearly articulates the expression of the dance and maintains its creative integrity. A very important part of this process is causing surprise by avoiding the predictable.

Insistence on accuracy and consistency of movement, concern for technique and style, panache and confidence, determination, provocation and ruthlessness, playful use of improvisation, accidents caused by juxtaposing, all contribute to the air of purpose and fun necessary to bring about satisfactory dance. In other words careful attention to detail.

Do not underestimate the value of numerical relationships between dancers in influencing the nature and substance of a dance. A solo is radically different from a trio which differs greatly from a sextet. It is a personal decision as to what constitutes a 'small group', and when such a gathering becomes a 'large group'. Within the concept of a large group the numerical possibilities are enormous for creating variety, producing the unpredictable, and for forwarding the intention of the choreography.

All choreographic forms are not rules as such but principles of composition. They are only of use and value if they are regarded as guidelines and not as a systematic code to be followed. The vast majority of dances created do not fall into any one of the established choreographic forms. Only by bending, breaking and taking risks with known principles is new ground broken and invention and innovation possible. However, choreographic conventions are useful to rest on when ideas run dry or the dance-maker is stuck for what to do next. They are a step on from improvisation, and understanding them enables improvisation to be regularised whether in solo or group form.

53 Motif – body

Motifs are many and varied. To make a motif means to get at the essence of an idea and express it very succinctly in a short movement phrase. Two or more motifs together will form a phrase. In turn, phrases put together form a sequence.

In creating a motif it is essential to explore the possibilities extensively.

This can only be done through improvisation. A motif can be varied by altering the:

– body activities – body parts in use;
– dynamics – rhythm, tempo;
– spatial placement – level, direction, pattern; and
– numbers dancing – formation and relationships.

Some motifs are best left in their original state. It is not always necessary to elaborate them but merely to repeat them. A statement in dance is very often more effective when it is simple and precise.

▶ Completely alone, create a very short piece of continuous movement that expresses:

– rise,
– sway,
– spin,
– grip.

With all four motifs get rid of any movement that does not contribute to the essence of the word.

▶ . . . Connect the four motifs in their most natural sequence.

54 Motif – space

The following should cause you to use and emphasise the use of space in different ways.

▶ Create a motif from the idea of 'happiness'.

▶ In contrast, create a motif from the idea of 'sadness'.

▶ Now establish a motif from the idea of 'fear'.

▶ Lastly, establish a motif from the idea of 'craziness'.

▶ Take *one* of these four ideas. Improvise much more broadly on the idea in general, regularly returning to and performing the motif already created for the idea.

▶ Find ways of connecting the four motifs so that they run from happiness to sadness to fear to craziness.

▶ Amongst the group, look at how many different motifs have been produced to communicate the same four ideas.

55 *Motif – dynamics*

▶ Explore through improvisation the following three dance characteristics:

- slow, gentle, day dreaming;
- quick, lively, exuberant;
- strong, forceful, dominant.

▶ Establish a motif for each one.

▶ Take *one* of the motifs and by varying it, create a short dance to further develop the expression of the character.

▶ Work with a partner who has taken the same character for his/her dance and create a duet (perhaps even interchange motifs).

▶ By finding the appropriate dancers, that is three of you, make a dance linking all three characters one after the other.

▶ Finish the dance by repeating your character dance at exactly the same time and in the same space as the others. Thus the dance runs:

daydreaming – solo
exuberant – solo
dominant – solo
all three together

▶ Finally, put three different duets together at the same time. Experiment with placement, position, and spacing until relationships are brought about.

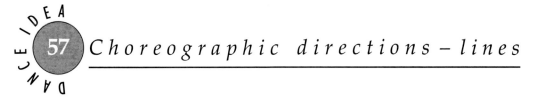

56 Motif – themes

▶ Take the possibilities apparent in 'dashes and dots' and create a motif.

▶ Use the feeling of curiosity to establish a motif.

▶ *'But I am slow of speech and of a slow tongue'*. Create a number of motifs for this theme.

▶ *Bowed by the weight of centuries he leans*
Upon his hoe and gazes on the ground,
The emptiness of ages in his face,
And on his back the burden of the world.

Edwin Markham

Explore what motifs could be brought about using these four lines of a poem.

▶ *'The words of his mouth were smoother than butter, but war was in his heart; his words were softer than oil, yet were they drawn swords.'*

Psalms LV.21.

Do the same with this quotation

▶ Using one of the ideas above, develop a short solo dance using the motif or motifs already created.

57 Choreographic directions – lines

▶ In small groups of five, six, seven or eight, thoroughly explore the use of a single file.

▶ The line can start, travel, stop. When still, the dancers can be in the same shape, or shapes can be alternated, or they can all be different. The line can move vertically (one after the other) or horizontally (side by side). It can travel straight or curve and snake. Directions or angles can be changed suddenly, as can levels, speed and so on.

▶ In groups of ten or twelve do the same with double file lines. (Everything possible with single file lines is possible with the double file. In addition there is the potential for meeting and parting, and going through.)

▶ In the groups of six, eights, tens or twelves connect the best single file and double file phrases into a finished sequence.

▶ In small groups work on what can be done with a circle. The circle can revolve clockwise and anti-clockwise. It can expand and contract, with and without a point of focus. It can travel in either direction whilst opening and closing. It can rise and fall. Body shapes and actions within it can be the same, alternate or be all different. They can be in unison, occur one after the other, change fronts and so on. The possibilities are many.

▶ Put two groups together, one inside the other, and explore what is possible with double circles and circles within circles.

▶ Ensure a short finished sequence capable of being shown to others.

▶ Create a circle dance based on the statement 'The nature of God is a circle of which the centre is everywhere and the circumference is nowhere'.

59 Choreographic directions –

interweaving

Single files, double files, circles and multiples of circles all have the potential for interweaving.

▶ In groups large enough to accommodate the task, find ways of forming and re-forming lines and circles using the idea of interweaving.

60 Choreographic directions –

group shapes

There are a variety of regular group shapes that can be formed when a group of dancers get together. The effect that they have and what they communicate depend on:

- the speed with which they form and disperse;
- the proximity of dancers, that is whether they are close or apart (and if so how far);
- the density of dancers;
- the level, direction, focus; and
- the shapes themselves.

The shapes are:

- rectangular block;
- triangle;
- line;
- semi-circle;
- circle;
- fan;
- zig-zag;
- spiral.

▶ Use two sets of ideas in all their possible combinations to explore what they have to offer.

▶ Form small groups – enough to cover all the group shapes. Each group takes two shapes, explores them and sets a sequence.

▶ Perform them on the floor at the same time.

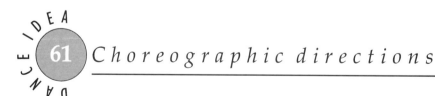

61 Choreographic directions

▶ In fairly large groups take the choreographic directions of lines, double lines, circles, multiples of circles, and interweaving together with the regular group shapes and create a finished dance ranging across all the ideas.

62 Choreographic form – binary

Binary form is often referred to as the AB form. It is essentially a simple short dance form in two parts, which contrast with each other but are linked through the initial stimulus. Very often the second part is developed from some fragment of movement contained in the first part.

Any task set in binary form should be done solo for the sake of establishing clarity. However when binary pieces have been achieved they can be moulded into group dances of limited duration.

▶ With masking tape, mark a meter square on the floor.

▶ Staying within the square and by using levels, fronts, diagonals, gestures, turning and, if possible, jumping, create a short Section A.

▶ Create Section B of the dance by leaving the square and travelling in the space around and beyond it. Do not re-enter the square until the very end of this sequence.

63 Choreographic form – ternary

Ternary form is described as an ABA dance. To explain, it consists of two contrasting sections, with the first being repeated immediately after the second. It is probably one of the most commonly used choreographic forms because it appears to be satisfyingly balanced. The form does allow the relationship of dancers to alter entirely (when in use with a group) and then return together again. It gives experience in unison work as well as independent expression. However, it is somewhat predictable.

▶ Find a short piece of music in ternary form or construct an original one from two entirely different music sources.

▶ Create a solo ternary dance allowing the music/sound to dictate the formation of motifs, phrases, and sequences.

▶ In trios, extend the solo work into a group ternary piece.

64 Choreographic form – rondo

The rondo form can be likened to a song which has contrasting verses interspersed by the repetitive chorus. The verses are quite different from each other but, as in ternary form, there is security to be found for the dancer, the choreographer and the audience in the familiarity of section A – the chorus. In the case of rondo, the form is ABACADA. This choreographic form is well suited to dances which involve changing relationships. In other words, the numbers of dancers can change from one section to another and the range of possibilities are endless. The most obvious examples of changing relationships in rondo form are the same as that which is to be found in the opera or the ballet, i.e. the chorus is sung or danced by a group, and the verses are performed by solo artists.

▶ Take as the stimulus for the dance the idea of contrasting 'gossip' with the need to be 'silent'. Gossip implies gabble and small-talk which can only happen in a group – so this can be the source of the 'A' theme, or chorus. Silence implies being alone or in solitude – so three different attitudes can be created in dance to express this and so themes B, C and D, or the verses, will be established.

▶ In groups of approximately nine, create and perfect the 'gossip' chorus.

▶ Individually, create a very short solo based on 'silence'. Make sure the solos are all approximately the same length.

▶ Organise three solos to emerge from the group at the end of the first statement/chorus of 'gossip'. Once performed the three dancers should return to the group. After the second and repeated 'gossip' chorus, three more emerge and return, and so on. The dance ends with a last 'gossip' chorus.

65 Choreographic form – canon

Canon form is a more difficult choreographic form to both understand and achieve. Music is the best analogy. The principle is that one instrument or voice starts a theme, a second instrument or voice joins in during that statement, then a third, and so on. But not indefinitely. A canon in dance can only carry a certain number of 'voices' before it becomes tedious or impossible to resolve. So, effectively this means that two, three or more instruments/voices/dancers are playing/singing/dancing different parts of the melody/theme, but in harmony. From a dance point of view it is imperative that the different parts of the theme are clearly defined so that they show sufficient contrast and yet are complementary to each other. The floor pattern must not entangle the dancers.

▶ In pairs, create a short dance in two parts. The first part should use turning, elevation and travel. This should contrast with the second part of the dance which should be on or around the spot where changes of level are important.

▶ Make sure the pairs can perform the short dance identically, exactly and in unison.

▶ Canon the dance at the change-over point, that is, both establish stillness with or without shape. One of the two begins the dance whilst the other remains still. As the one dancing ends the travel part and begins working on the spot, the other dancer begins the travel sequence. When the first dancer finishes they should be still, or whenever the second dancer begins the section on the spot, the first dancer could repeat and be in unison. Thus the canon is resolved.

▶ Make the canon much more difficult by containing four, five or six dancers within the two-part dance.

▶ Extend the complexity and interest of the canon work by using more than one canon motif and by increasing the number of dancers.

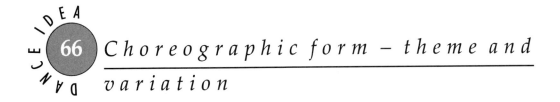

IDEA 66 Choreographic form – theme and variation

Theme and variation is not nearly as prescriptive, predictable, or as easy to execute as the other choreographic forms. It does allow for concentration on, and thorough exploration of, the development possibilities of a movement motif be this by change or repetition. Dancers of all abilities can use it in simple or complex form. The motif is created. Then any number of variations can be made according to the needs of the dance, but all should contain some aspect of the original.

▶ Given the theme of 'people together alone and people alone together', work in small groups to establish the motif or motifs that express/communicate the two major themes.

▶ Create variations to develop the dance to a conclusion, employing repetition where appropriate.

▶ A simple format might be:

    – meeting and parting;
    – linking and dividing;
    – uniting and moving as one.

67 *Angry and counting*

'When angry, count four, when very angry, swear.'
Samuel L. Clements

▶ Think very carefully about this phrase.

▶ Do not plan to do the obvious.

▶ Find a way of dealing with the idea of swearing that will not offend.

▶ Create a dance either in solo, duo, or small group format.

68 *Choose*

The single clenched fist, lifted and ready,
Or the open asking hand, held out and waiting.
Choose.
For we meet by one or the other.
Carl Sanberg

▶ Create a duet based on this quotation.

▶ 'Crowd' – explore the possibilities in this word and create a group dance.

Crabbit Old Woman

This poem was found amongst the possessions of an old Irish lady who died in a geriatric hospital.

What do you see nurses, what do you see,
What are you thinking, when you look at me?
A crabbit old woman, not very wise,
Uncertain of habit, with far-away eyes,
Who dribbles her food, and makes no reply.
When you say in a loud voice, 'I do wish you'd try'.
Who seems not to notice the things that you do,
And forever is loving a stocking or shoe,
Who, unresisting or not, let's you do as you will,
With bathing and feeding, the long day to fill.
Is that what you're thinking, is that what you see?
Then open your eyes, you're not looking at me.
I'll tell you who I am as I sit here so still,
As I move at your bidding, as I eat at your will.
I'm a small child of ten with father and mother,
Brothers and sisters who love one another,
A young girl at sixteen with wings on her feet,
Dreaming that soon now a lover she'll meet.
A bride soon at twenty – my heart gives a leap,
Remembering the vows that I promised to keep.
At twenty-five now I have young of my own,
Who need me to build a secure happy home.
A woman of thirty my young now grow fast,
Bound to each other with ties that should last.
At forty my young now will soon be gone,
But my man stays beside me to see I don't mourn.
At fifty once more babies play round my knee,
Again we know children, my loved one and me.
Dark days are upon me, my husband is dead,
I look at the future, I shudder with dread,
For my young are all busy rearing young of their own,
And I think of the years and the love I have known.
I'm an old woman now and nature is cruel,
'tis her jest to make old age look like a fool.
The body it crumbles, grace and vigour depart,
And now there's a stone where I once had a heart.
But inside this old carcass a young girl still dwells,
And now and again my battered heart swells,
I remember the joys, I remember the pain,
And I'm loving and living life over again.

I think of the years all too few – gone so fast,
And accept the stark fact that nothing can last.
So open your eyes nurses, open and see,
Not a crabbit old woman, look closer – see me.

▶ Create what is essentially a solo dance but do not be afraid to involve other dancers in 'back-drop' work.

71 Christmas Eve

Seek out a copy of the recording of Charpentier's *Midnight Mass for Christmas Eve*. Take the following sections:

– Kyrie: Gloria and Amen
– Credo
– Sanctus
– Agnus Dei
– Exultate

▶ After researching the several different versions of the nativity story create a group dance.

72 Colours Speak

'Blue is true,
Yellow's jealous,
Green's forsaken,
Red's brazen,
White is love,
And black is death' . . .
            Anon

▶ There is enormous potential in the association of colours and emotions. Create a dance.

73 Casting off

Hindu philosophy quotes the following:

> *As a man casts off his worn-out clothes*
> *And takes on other new ones (in their place)*
> *So does the embodied soul cast off his*
> *worn out bodies*
> *And enters others new.*

▶ Create a dance.

74 Bats

The following is quoted from the poem *Bat* by D.H. Lawrence.

> *Little lumps that fly in air and have voices indefinite, wildly*
> *   vindictive;*
>
> *Wings like bits of umbrella.*
>
> *Bats!*
>
> *Creatures that hang themselves up like an old rag, to sleep;*
> *And disgustingly upside down.*
> *Hanging upside down like rows of disgusting old rags*
> *And grinning in their sleep.*
> *Bats!*
>
> *In China the bat is a symbol of happiness.*
>
> *Not for me!*

▶ Record a spoken version of the poem.

▶ Create a short solo using the recorded poem.

▶ In a group, create a dance based on the poem but do not use the recorded poem or have it spoken out loud.

75 Growl and mumble

Growling	Mumbling
Hissing	Squeaking
Humming	Croaking
Whining	Clicking
Sobbing	Whistling
Laughing	Shouting
Sneezing	Whispering

▶ Take one group of words only, as the source of the dance.

▶ Do not use the words as words; the sounds *suggested* by the words must be used.

▶ Create a group dance.

▶ Stimulated by the Bretecher cartoon below, create a group dance called 'The Dog Dirt Dance'.

...and that was Wayne Fonteyn in an extract from 'Dog Days', choreographed by Kenneth Ashton at the Camden Dance Floor...

until July 14

Echoes

*Some madman shrieking on the mountain top, on hearing the
echo from below may go to see it in the valley.
Once in the valley he shrieks again and straightaway
climbs to search back among the peaks.
Such a man may spend a thousand rebirths searching
for the source of these sounds by following their
echoes.
Far better that you make no sound, for then there will
be no echo and you will be one with the dwellers in
Nirvana.*

Anon

► Using the ancient Chinese proverb quoted above, create a duet in
three sections.

78 Fog

Curling and writhing, slowly
Enveloping all in its billowing mass, coldly,
Slowly it creeps on, and on,
Till none can see anything but fog.

Slowly it descends, a cloud,
Upon a lawn, or city,
Making all look grey, and sad,
But it goes as it comes, slowly.

Francis Horner

▶ Create a short dance to the poem as it is spoken.

▶ Create a longer dance using the ideas in the poem but do not accompany the finished dance with the poem.

▶ Find an appropriate piece of music (for instance Bo Hannsons' 'Fog on the Borrow Downs' from the LP *'Lord of the Rings'*) and create a group dance using the theme of fog from the poem.

79 Fragments

▶ Explore the following as sources of ideas for solo work:

  – the sound of laughter;
  – rocking chair;
  – fragment of a ballet;
  – electricity;
  – departure for a voyage;
  – child at play.

▶ Having improvised each, use the one that appeals the most and create a dance.

▶ The illustration by Gerald Scarfe has fourteen different movement
images. Take seven each and create a duet.

81 Food

► Create a duet based on favourite foods. For instance, the dance could be called 'Sausages, chips and ice-cream' or 'Jam and jelly' or 'Bangers and mash' or 'Bubble and squeak' or 'pop–corn'.

82 Newspaper

A newspaper or magazine is an interesting object as a source of ideas for dance. They can be used alone, in pairs or in groups.

► Choose a headline and create a dance.

► Find an interesting story and create a dance.

► Take a photograph as the stimulus for a dance.

► Dance the advertisement.

► During the course of a dance do one or more of the following, making sure that it is appropriate to the dance and not just using it as a gimmick.

– read it;
– roll it up;
– tear it up;
– crumple it;
– spread it out;
– strike out with it;
– wave it.

83 Punctuate the idea

Take the following idea: 'Squaring the circle, stopping the comma, and cutting a dash.'

► Create a dance together as a group.

84 Praying hands

Find a copy of the etching *Praying Hands* by Albrecht Dürer.

▶ Discuss what is being expressed.

▶ Explore through improvisation the use of the hands.

▶ Create a solo dance where the use of hands dominates the action and where the repeated motif is the hands in the praying position.

85 Silent night

Find and record the version of *Silent Night* as sung by Simon and Garfunkel. (No other version will do.)

▶ Create a duet where one dancer works to the music and the words of the song and the other dancer works to the background material.

86 Prisoners

Research the theme of prisoners. It is particularly well expressed by Stephen Spendor in his poem *The Prisoners* and by the following anonymous quote:

'. . . people look through iron bars. One see darkness and others stars.'

▶ Create a group dance, with or without poetic and/or music accompaniment.

87 Simon – a view to death

Read Chapter 9, 'A View to a Death', from *Lord of the Flies* by William Golding.

▶ Create a group dance that tells the story of this chapter.

▶ Use the following words during the course of the dance: 'Kill the beast! Cut his throat! Spill his blood!'

Properties hold a vast store of dance potential for solo, duet, trio, small and large group work.

▶ Select one, or try all of the ones offered below:

- suitcase;
- broom;
- gown;
- sponge;
- rope;
- tailors dummy;
- hat;
- cushion;
- bucket;
- flowers;
- pole;
- ball;
- stool;
- dictionary;
- telephone directory.

89 *Many cannot many do*

Many can argue; not many converse.

Alcott

▶ Create a group dance based on this quotation.

90 *Maze*

'Going through a maze'.

▶ Explore the possibilities of this phrase and create a group dance.

91 Protest

The following is much quoted:

> *When they came for the Jews I was not a Jew, so I did not protest,*
> *When they came for the Communists, I was not a Communist, so I did not protest,*
> *When they came for the trade unionist, I was not a trade unionist, so I did not protest;*
> *When they came for me there was nobody left to protest.*
>
> Pastor Martin Niemoller

▶ Find out information about the persecution of the Jews throughout history.

▶ Reflect on the nature of communism, its effect and the changes that have occurred/are occurring.

▶ Consider the nature of trade unions and their history.

▶ Create a dance from the quotation.

92 Rhythm of life

In the Bible, Ecclesiastes, Chapter 3, Verse 1, it says: 'To everything there is a season and a time to every purpose under heaven.'

A suite of dances can result from this quotation. They could be:

– a time of birth;
– a time of play;
– a time of work;
– a time of war;
– a time of grief;
– a time to dance.

▶ Create the dance.

93 Diamond

▶ Identify the characteristic shape, texture, colour and form of a diamond.

▶ As a group use the ideas to create a dance.

94 Walkin', jumpin', fallin'

▶ Compose a dance as a solo, duet or trio based on the ideas of:

- sad walks;
- angry jumps;
- funny falls.

95 *The wise are still, the knowing move*

To move when all around is still attracts attention. Remaining still when all around is movement creates a barrier. Knowing when to move and when to stay still is the essence of true wisdom.

(From the 'stars' column of a magazine.)

▶ Create a group dance.

96 *We surround*

▶ Take the idea 'We surround, we lift, we split, we travel, we merge, we surround' and find appropriate sound/music as accompaniment.

▶ Create a group dance.

97 Thoughts

The following words must be kept in the order given:

- march;
- repose;
- wandering.

▶ As a group, create a dance exploring these words according to their strict definition.

▶ Try to find a suitable piece of music in three parts;

or

find three separate pieces to record one after the other. If there are pauses between the pieces of music these should be put to use in the dance.

98 Week days

The days of the week have been renamed and now read as follows:

- Moonsday
- Tearsday
- Wailsday
- Thumpsday
- Frightday
- Shatterday
- Shunday

(Reproduced with the permission of Katherine Lee)

▶ Create a group dance.

Noon, and hazy heat;
A single silver slither and dull drone;
The gloved finger poised, pressed:
A second's silence and
Oblivion.

Anon

This short verse about Hiroshima so poignantly sets the scene for the awful aftermath of such an horrific action.

▶ Use the image of the gloved finger as the start and finish point of the dance.

▶ Find appropriate music or sound – something like *Fonogrammi* by Krztof Penderecki.

▶ Create the dance.

Conclusion

The larger part of this book has been concerned with offering ideas of quality so that the philosophy, practice and art of dance in education might be encouraged. Relevant theory, in limited form, was offered where appropriate, but the book unapologetically assumes a basic level of knowledge and understanding on the part of the teacher but not necessarily the students.

Because there is little reference to the need for research, reflection and critical awareness, it should not be assumed that these areas of activity are considered unimportant or have been ignored. It is worth the reminder that the intention of the book was that of suggesting and not dictating; that the ideas offered should be the touch paper of possibilities. Some of the ideas represent only a foot in the door of a given area of exploration and study, and it would be patronising of us to attempt to tell you everything and how to do it. Improvisation, composition and performance are inherent to the process and content of any dance activity. All dance activities contribute to the appreciation of dance. The expectation we have of you as the teacher is as high as the expectation level we have suggested you should have of your students. The only way to quantify the expectation is through analysis, reflection and criticism – in other words evaluation.

The appreciation of dance is a vibrant, participatory activity. It is not passive and need not just take the written form; there are many ways of documenting appreciation other than consigning it to the written page. Dance is essentially a performing art with a visual dimension. Its emotional power and intellectual impact cannot be contained in the writing on the page nor can its essence be communicated through the reading of a book. Dance has to be seen to be properly responded to, whether that be actual or through the secondary medium of the screen. There are a number of questions that can be asked to evaluate dance/dance activity, but since there are in reality no rules of choreography then it is not necessary to draw specific conclusions nor establish definitive answers:

> Is the intention of the dance clearly communicated? How?
> Does the dance hold the watcher's interest? Why?
> Is the movement inventive? In what way?
> Can the movement be anticipated or is there an element of surprise? How has this been achieved?
> Is there rhythmic organisation which is apparent? How has this been used?
> Do the movement relationships seem fresh or new? For what reasons?

Does the dance hold together as a whole? Explain why.
Is the problem effectively solved?

There are a number of criteria involved here which may equally cause thought, exploration and examination. They are:

Content.
Unity of structure.
Originality of movement.
Spatial interest.
Dynamic quality.
Rhythmic value.
Relationships.
Performance quality.

Many aesthetic attributes are essential to effective dance communication. On this point, and as a fitting conclusion we are given to remembering that:

It is only when all factors of an image, all their individual effects, are completely attuned to the one intrinsic vital feeling that is expressed in the whole – when, so to speak, the clarity of the image coincides with the clarity of the inner content – that a truly artistic form is achieved.
(*From On the Problems of Artistic Form* by Paul Stern.)

If the ideas in this book have contributed to or allowed for this possibility in any way, then the job has been well done.

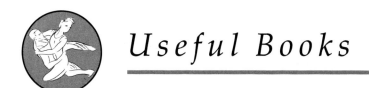

Useful Books

Dance Books

4–7 Years (Approx)

Look! Look! What I Can Do!, Kate Harrison. BBC Books.

7–13 Years (Approx)

Bright Ideas – Dance and Movement, Kate Harrison, Jane Layton and Melanie Morris. Scholastic.

Children Dancing, Rosamund Shreeves. Wardlock.

11–16 Years (Approx)

A Primer For Choreographers, Lois Ellfeldt. National Press Publications Corporation.

14–19+ Years (Approx)

The Intimate Act of Choreography, Lynne Anne Blom and L. Tarin Chaplin University of Pittsburgh Press.

16–19+ Years (Approx)

New Dance – Approaches to Non-Literal Choreography, Margery J. Turner. University of Pittsburgh Press.

Poetry Books

3–11 Years (Approx)

That Way and This – Poetry for Creative Dance, Frances Baldwin and Margaret Whitehead. Chatto Windus.
A Puffin Quartet of Poets, Kaye Webb (ed.). Penguin.
Rhyme and Rhythm – Blue Book, Gibson and Wilson. Macmillan.
Roundabout Six, Margaret Rawlins and Frederick Warne.
There's Motion Everywhere, John Travers. Nelson.

Junior Voices 1–4, Geoffrey Summerfield. Penguin Edition.
Wordscapes, Barry Maybury. Oxford University Press.
Complete Poems for Children, James Reeves. Heinemann.
Poems to Hear and See, Ian Hamilton. Finlay Macmillan.
A Book of Milliganimals, Spike Milligan. Puffin.
Fire Words, Christopher Searle. Jonathan Cape.
Tower Blocks – Poems of the City, Marion Lines. Franklin Watts.
Peep Show – A Little Book of Rhymes, Pamela Blake. Longman.
This Little Puffin, Elizabeth Matterson. Puffin.
Mother Goose, Brian Wildsmith. Oxford University Press.

General Books

The Art and Science of Creativity, George F. Kneller. Holt Rinehart and Winston.
The Foundation of Language, Andrew Wilkinson. Oxford University Press.
Knowing in My Bones, Ruth Foster. A & C Black.
Movement Awareness and Creativity, Lea Bartal and Nira Neeman. Souvenir Press.
The Arts in Schools, Calouste Gulbenkian. Foundation.
Arts 5-16 A Curriculum Framework. Longman/NFAE.
Living Power, Peter Abbs. Longman.
A is for Aesthetic, Peter Abbs. Longman.
Non-verbal Communication, Robert A. Hinde (ed.). Cambridge University Press.

Acknowledgments

Photographs and illustrations have been taken from the classwork and choreography of John Auty.

Poems on pages 24, 33, 42 and 43 provided by Kate Harrison.

Photographers: Graham Carver and Peter Huggins.
Photographic lighting: Bryan Smith.
Dancers: Pupils of Intake High School, Leeds.

The authors and publishers would like to thank the following for permission to use material in this book:

Bantam Doubleday Dell for three extracts from *Best Quotations for all Occasions* edited by Lewis C. Henry; Chatto & Windus for the poem 'Fog' by Frances Horner from *That Way and This – Poetry for Creative Dance*; Methuen London for the Cartoon from *Frustration* by Claire Bretecher; Gerald Scarfe for the illustration 'Dancin'; Viking Penguin, a division of Penguin Books USA Inc. for 'Bat' from *The Complete Poems of D.H. Lawrence* by D.H. Lawrence Eds. de sola Pinto & Roberts. Copyright © 1964, 1971 by Angelo Ravagli & C.M. Weekley, executors of the Estate of Frieda Lawrence Ravalgi; Atheneum Publishers (Macmillan Publishing Company) for the poem 'Go Wind' by Lilian Moore from *'I fell the same way'*. Copyright © 1967.